# THE WINTER OLYMPICS

Nick Hunter

Raintree is an imprint of Capstone Global Library Limited, a company incorporated in England and Wales having its registered office at 7 Pilgrim Street, London, EC4V 6LB – Registered company number: 6695582

To contact Raintree, please phone 0845 6044371, fax + 44 (0) 1865 312263, or email myorders@raintreepublishers.co.uk.

Text © Capstone Global Library Limited 2014
First published in hardback in 2014
Paperback edition first published in 2014
The moral rights of the proprietor have been asserted.

Edited by Nick Hunter and Diyan Leake
Designed by Steve Mead
Original illustrations © Capstone Global Library Ltd 2014
Picture research by Ruth Blair
Production by Victoria Fitzgerald
Originated by Capstone Global Library Ltd
Printed and bound in China by CTPS

ISBN 978 1 406 26171 4 (hardback)
17 16 15 14 13
10 9 8 7 6 5 4 3 2 1

ISBN 978 1 4062 6173 8 (paperback)
17 16 15 14 13
10 9 8 7 6 5 4 3 2 1

**British Library Cataloguing in Publication Data**
Hunter, Nick
The Winter Olympics.
A full catalogue record for this book is available from the British Library.

**Acknowledgements**
We would like to thank the following for permission to reproduce photographs: Corbis pp. 19 (© Claus Fisker/EPA), 27 (© Anastasia Mishchenko/Demotix); Getty Images pp. 4 (Clive Rose), 5 (Cameron Spencer), 6 (IOC, Olympic Museum/Allsport), 7 (Hulton Archive), 8 (Bob Thomas), 9 (Bongarts), 10 (Kevork Djansezian), 11 (Richard Heathcote), 12 (Jonathan Nackstrand/AFP), 13 (Alberto Pizzoli/AFP), 14 (Clive Mason), 15 (Georges Gobet/AFP), 16 (Robyn Beck/AFP), 17 (Matthew Stockman), 18 (Bruce Bennett), 20 (Adrian Dennis/AFP), 21 (Doug Pensinger), 22 (Jaime L. Mikle), 23 (Jamie McDonald), 25 (Clive Brunskill), 26 (Daniel Slim/AFP).

Cover photograph of Shaun White of the United States in the finals of the men's half-pipe snowboarding competition during the Torino 2006 Winter Olympic Games reproduced courtesy of Corbis (© K.C. Alfred/SDU-T/ZUMA).

Every effort has been made to contact copyright holders of material reproduced in this book. Any omissions will be rectified in subsequent printings if notice is given to the publisher.

# Contents

Winter wonderland ........................................ 4

The first Winter Olympics.......................... 6

The changing Winter Games ..................... 8

Symbols and ceremonies ...................... 10

Supreme skiers.......................................... 12

Going downhill fast.................................. 14

On the ice.................................................... 16

Terrific teams.............................................. 18

Extreme winter sports ............................. 20

Winter Paralympics ................................. 22

Controversy at the Games ..................... 24

Sochi 2014 ................................................ 26

Winter Olympic factfile .......................... 28

Glossary........................................................ 30

Find out more ............................................ 31

Index .............................................................. 32

Some words are shown in bold, **like this.** You can find out what they mean by looking in the glossary.

# Winter wonderland

The skier has trained for four years for this moment. In a few seconds, he will plunge down the mountain at speeds of up to 135 kilometres (85 miles) per hour. In less than two minutes, if he can avoid a high-speed crash, the skier will know whether he has achieved his goal. Will he have what it takes to become the Winter Olympic champion?

Downhill skiers travel faster than a speeding car, with very little to protect them from injury if they crash.

The Winter Olympics are the ultimate sporting event for snow and ice athletes. Every four years, thousands of skiers, skaters, and sliders test their skills against the best in the world. Often, they are also testing themselves against the natural landscape and weather conditions that are the backdrop for many winter sports.

# Speed, skill, and snow

The Winter Olympics include some of the world's fastest and most dangerous sports, from downhill skiing to luge. Skill and constant practice are the keys to success in figure skating and the amazing tricks of freestyle skiers and snowboarders.

## THE OLYMPIC MOVEMENT

"The goal of the **Olympic Movement** is to contribute to building a peaceful and better world by educating youth through sport practised in accordance with Olympism and its values."

From the Olympic Charter. The Winter Olympic Games, like the Summer Games, are organized by the **International Olympic Committee (IOC)** and the Olympic Movement.

Skiers race head to head around a twisting, bumpy course in the thrilling sport of ski-cross.

# The first Winter Olympics

The first winter sport event to take place at the Olympics was in London in 1908, when figure skating was included in the games. In 1912, Stockholm in Sweden was the host city of the Olympics. The **IOC** tried to persuade the Swedes to stage a winter event as well. They refused, believing that winter Olympic Games would damage their own Nordic Games.

The Chamonix Games were only officially called the first Winter Olympic Games in 1926.

PARIS - LYON - MEDITERRANEE

AUX VAINQUEURS DU CONCOURS DE LA VIIIᵐᵉ OLYMPIADE

CHAMONIX. MONT-BLANC

25 Janvier-5 Février 1924

## OLYMPIC FACTFILE: CHAMONIX 1924

Countries: 16

Athletes: 247 men, 11 women

Most successful country: Norway

- American speed-skater Charles Jewtraw became the first Winter Olympic gold medallist.
- 11-year-old Norwegian skater Sonja Henie failed to win a medal in Chamonix. She won three golds at later Games and went on to become a film star.

The idea was discussed again after World War I, and the IOC agreed to hold a "Winter Sports Week" in Chamonix, France in 1924. More than 10,000 spectators made the event a big success. Norway and Sweden topped the **medal table**, but Canada were unstoppable in the ice hockey competition. The Winter Olympics were here to stay.

The United States' speed skaters practise on the ice at the 1924 Winter Olympics.

## BOBSLEIGH BEGINNINGS

The first bobsleighs were created in the 1880s by fixing two **toboggans** together. The rules for bobsleigh competition were only agreed a few days before the Olympics started!

# The changing Winter Games

The Winter Olympics have changed constantly since 1924. By 2010, more than 2,500 athletes from 82 countries were competing at the Games. The athletes' incredible skills are now watched by a huge television audience around the world.

Ice skaters Jayne Torvill and Christopher Dean won gold at the 1984 Sarajevo Winter Olympics.

The Winter Olympics were held every four years from 1924 until 1992, apart from a break during World War II. By 1992, the cost and effort of holding the Winter Olympics in the same year as the Summer Olympics was too great. The next Games in Lillehammer, Norway, were held two years later in 1994. Since then, the Winter and Summer Olympics have been held two years apart.

## Slippery slopes

Problems for the Winter Olympics have included too much or too little snow and ice. Only a relatively small number of countries can stage such a huge winter-sports event, but the Games have been held in Europe, North America, and Asia.

## VIKING GOLD

The all-time Winter Olympics **medal table** is topped by Norway, a nation of less than 5 million people. Norway won the most medals at five of the first six Winter Olympics. Even in 2010, Norway won nine gold medals, equalling the United States.

Norway's Bjørn Dæhlie is the most successful Winter Olympic champion of all time. He has won 12 medals, including eight golds in the gruelling sport of cross-country skiing.

# Symbols and ceremonies

Olympic symbols are at the heart of the **Olympic Movement**. Many of these symbols look back to the ancient Olympic Games held by the ancient Greeks from around 776 BC. These Games were the model for the modern Olympic Games, although they never included winter sports.

Every Winter Olympic Games begins with an opening ceremony. The opening ceremony includes music and culture from the host country as well as a parade of athletes. During the opening ceremony, the Olympic flame will be lit. The flame burns throughout the Games. The Olympic flag of five interlocking rings also flies during the Games. Its five rings represent the five areas of the world competing at the Games.

The 2010 Winter Olympics in Vancouver, Canada began with a spectacular opening ceremony.

# Torch relay

Before each Winter Olympics, an Olympic torch is lit at Olympia in Greece. The torch is carried across the host country in a relay before it is used to light the Olympic flame at the opening ceremony. In 2010, the torch travelled 45,000 kilometres (28,000 miles) across Canada in 106 days.

## OLYMPIC MASCOTS

**Mascots** have been part of the Winter Olympics ever since the Games in Innsbruck, Austria in 1976. The Austrian mascot was a snowman with a traditional Austrian hat. The official mascot is often an animal from the host country. Recent Games, such as Vancouver 2010, have included several mascots to represent different features of the Games or the host country.

Ice hockey legend Wayne Gretzky lit the Olympic flame at the 2010 Opening Ceremony.

# Supreme skiers

Alpine skiing is one of the Winter Olympics' most exciting sports. The downhill champion is the fastest man or woman on two skis. Skiing is so popular, it seems amazing that the sport was not part of the Winter Olympics until 1936.

Skiers compete in downhill, super G, giant slalom, and slalom. Super G combines the electric pace of downhill with tighter turns through gates. Slalom is all about keeping control all the way down the course.

## Nordic skiing

Nordic cross-country skiers race over distances up to 50 kilometres (31 miles). They are some of the world's fittest endurance athletes.

### LINDSEY VONN

US skiing star Lindsey Vonn was happier than most athletes when the downhill skiing was delayed by bad weather in Vancouver in 2010. The delay gave her time to recover from injury and ski to her first gold medal

Sky-scraping ski jumpers are judged on style as well as how far they jump.

## OLYMPIC FACTFILE: TORINO 2006

Countries: 80

Athletes: 1548 men, 960 women

Most successful country: Germany

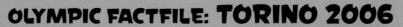

• Kjetil André Aamodt of Norway became the first skier to win four gold medals in a 14 year Olympic career.

• Half an hour later, Croatia's Janica Kostelić became the first woman to win four golds when she won the Alpine skiing event.

# Going downhill fast

Bobsleigh, skeleton, and luge are sliding events. They are some of the most thrilling and dangerous sports at the Games. Teams or individuals hurtle down an icy track at high speed, steering the best line through the steep corners to finish in the fastest time.

## SLEIGH RIDE

The first bobsleighs were made of wood. Today they are made of **streamlined fibreglass** over a metal frame. This offers some protection for the athletes. The driver steers by pulling ropes attached to **runners** at the front. Luge sleds are lightweight with no protection for athletes. Skeleton sliders hurtle down the track head first.

Getting a fast start is important in sliding events. Vancouver gold medallist Amy Williams was a runner before she took up the skeleton.

# Vancouver tragedy

Lugers hurtle down the same track as the bobsleigh at speeds of around 140 kilometres (90 miles) per hour. At Vancouver in 2010, Georgian luge athlete Nodar Kumaritashvili paid the ultimate price for his sport. He was killed when he crashed during a practice run on the day of the Games' opening ceremony.

## ICE COOL IN CALGARY

One of the most popular teams at the 1988 Calgary Winter Olympics was from a tropical island with no history of winter sports success. The Jamaican bobsleigh team did not challenge Switzerland for the gold medal but they made many friends and went on to compete at several Winter Olympics.

# On the ice

Skating has been part of the Olympic Games since before the Winter Olympics even started. Individual skaters and pairs make their intricate spins and turns look easy, but they also have to bring a lot of creativity to their routines. Any tiny mistake will be picked up by the judges.

## SHORT-TRACK SMASH

Steven Bradbury of Australia was in last place in the final of the 1000-metre short-track at the 2002 Winter Olympics when the skaters in front of him collided. Bradbury swept through to take gold.

Kim Yu-Na is one of South Korea's greatest sporting heroes after her gold medal in figure skating at the 2010 Winter Olympics.

# Super speed skaters

Speed skaters race at speeds of around 95 kilometres (60 miles) per hour. Each race features two skaters. Their skates are very different from those used by figure skaters, with longer blades helping them to go faster.

Short-track speed skating has been included at the Winter Olympics since 1992. The course is shorter, with tighter turns, and four skaters race at once. Crashes are common in this action-packed sport.

## APOLO OHNO

Short-track speed skater Apolo Ohno has won more Winter Olympic medals than any other American, with two gold, two silver, and four bronze medals. As well as shining on the ice, he also won the TV show *Dancing with the Stars* in 2007, before winning three medals at the Vancouver 2010 games.

# Terrific teams

The ultimate team sport at the Winter Olympics is ice hockey. The sport has been part of the Games since the Antwerp Summer Olympics of 1920. Women's ice hockey was not added to the Olympic programme until 1998, which was the same year that **professional** players in the National Hockey League (NHL) first appeared.

Events on ice have seen fierce rivalries between the United States and the **Soviet Union** during the decades after World War II, and more recently between Canada and the United States.

## SIDNEY CROSBY

Sidney Crosby was tipped for greatness from a young age. After a string of NHL honours, Crosby's greatest Olympic moment came in 2010. He scored the goal that brought victory over the United States in the final, and the gold medal that all of Canada had hoped for.

## OLYMPIC FACTFILE: VANCOUVER 2010

Countries: 82

Athletes: 1522 men, 1044 women

Most successful country: Canada

- Canada topped the **medal table** for the first time.
- The final of the men's ice hockey was the most-watched TV event in Canadian history. Canada also won gold in the women's ice hockey.

# Curlers in the house

Curling is team sport played at a slower pace. Each four-person team has to slide a large stone weighing nearly 20 kilograms (44 pounds) across the ice to an area called the house.

Curling team members brush the ice in front of the stone to help it slide further.

# Extreme winter sports

Winter sports have changed constantly since the Winter Olympics began in 1924. New materials and safety equipment have made sports like alpine skiing safer. They have also helped in the development of thrilling new sports, including snowboarding and freestyle skiing.

Snowboarding has become one of the most popular Olympic sports since the first competition in 1998. Athletes compete in slalom, snowboard-cross, slopestyle, and the spectacular **halfpipe**.

## Going aerial

Freestyle skiers perform in aerials, slopestyle, halfpipe, and moguls events. In the moguls event, they must combine speed over a bumpy course with a series of tricks. The tragic death of freestyle halfpipe skier Sarah Burke in 2012 was a grim reminder that athletes often take big risks to compete at the highest level.

### Shaun White

Shaun "The Flying Tomato" White is a legend of snowboarding with two Olympic gold medals in the halfpipe event. At the Vancouver Olympics, White performed a double McTwist 1260, a trick that only he could perform. Will he claim a third gold in 2014?

# NEW TRICKS

The 2014 Winter Olympics in Sochi, Russia will include several new events, including ski halfpipe and both ski and snowboard slopestyle. Athletes in slopestyle events will do a series of moves including grabs, grinds, and spins along a course packed with jumps and obstacles.

Athletes will be competing in the first Olympic ski halfpipe event at Sochi 2014.

# Winter Paralympics

Hot on the heels of the Winter Olympics come the Winter **Paralympics**. The incredible athletes at these Games have each overcome a disability to compete at the highest level. The first Winter Paralympics were held in 1976. Since 1992, Paralympic athletes have shared the sporting arenas used for the Winter Olympics a few weeks earlier.

## Paralympic sports

Sports at the Winter Paralympics include alpine and cross-country skiing, ice sledge hockey, and wheelchair curling. The **biathlon** competition combines cross-country skiing with rifle shooting. Races in different classifications mean that athletes compete against others with similar disabilities.

Ice sledge hockey is like ice hockey but, instead of skates, players use sledges to move around the ice.

Alpine skiers use different equipment. Amputees may use a single ski or **prosthetic** arms or legs. Visually impaired athletes ski with sighted skiers who guide them down the mountain.

## PARALYMPIC FACTFILE: VANCOUVER 2010

Countries: 44

Athletes: 502

Most successful country: Germany

- Athletes represented more countries than ever before.
- More tickets were sold than at any previous Winter Paralympics.

## LAUREN WOOLSTENCROFT

The Canadian athlete Lauren Woolstencroft was just four years old when she started skiing, despite being born missing both legs below the knee and her left arm below the elbow. In 2010, Woolstencroft won an amazing five gold medals in alpine skiing.

# Controversy at the Games

Controversy is never far from the world's biggest sporting events. The Winter Olympics are no exception.

One of the biggest scandals happened before the 1994 Games, when the husband of US skater Tonya Harding was accused of organizing an attack on her rival Nancy Kerrigan. Kerrigan recovered to win a silver medal at the Winter Olympics in Lillehammer, Norway, while Harding finished in eighth place.

## Drug cheats

Winter Olympic officials have to be on their guard against athletes using drugs that improve their performance. Drug cheats who have been caught at the Winter Olympics have often been competing in endurance events such as cross-country skiing.

### OLYMPIC FACTFILE: SALT LAKE CITY 2002

Countries: 77

Athletes: 1513 men, 886 women

Most successful country: Germany

- Ten **IOC** members resigned or were expelled for accepting **bribes** in return for their votes from cities bidding for the 2002 Games.

- Athletes from 18 countries won gold, including short-track speed skater Yang Yang (A), the first Chinese Winter Olympic Champion.

The Russian and Canadian pairs show off their shared gold medals at the 2002 Winter Olympics.

## SKATING SCANDAL

Winning and losing in figure skating depends on the votes of judges. In 2002, the judges awarded gold to a pair of Russian skaters. Most people watching thought the Canadian pair had deserved to win. In the end, a second set of gold medals was awarded to the Canadians. The judging system for skating was changed to prevent similar problems in future.

# Sochi 2014

Staging the Winter Olympics is a great honour and a huge project for any city. The host city is decided by members of the **IOC**. In 2014, the world's best snow and ice athletes will compete in the Winter Olympics in Sochi, Russia.

The venues for the Sochi Winter Olympics have been specially built for the Games, including skating venues and an Olympic Stadium beside the Black Sea.

The Iceberg Skating Palace will host the figure skating and short-track speed skating events at the Sochi Games.

# The world is watching

Some Winter Olympic stars will return to amaze us, and new stars will be launched. Once again the world's attention will be focused on the incredible Winter Olympics.

## OLYMPIC FACTFILE: SOCHI 2014

- The first time any Olympic Games have been held in Russia. (The 1980 Summer Olympics were staged in Moscow but Russia was part of the **Soviet Union** at that time.)
- Organizers plan to store 250,000 cubic metres of snow just in case there is not enough natural snow. They will also use more than 400 machines to make **artificial** snow.

## RUSSIA'S MASCOT TALENT

Sochi's official Olympic **mascots** are a snowboarding snow leopard, a hare, and a polar bear. They were selected by public vote on a live television show.

# Winter Olympic factfile

## Winter Olympic sports

Athletes will compete in the following sports at the Sochi Winter Olympics in 2014.

| | |
|---|---|
| Alpine skiing | Biathlon |
| Bobsleigh | Cross-country skiing |
| Curling | Figure skating |
| Freestyle skiing | Ice hockey |
| Luge | Nordic combined skiing |
| Short-track speed skating | Skeleton bobsleigh |
| Ski jumping | Snowboarding |

## Winter Olympics medal table

This **medal table** includes results from 1924 to 2010.

| Country | Gold | Silver | Bronze |
|---|---|---|---|
| Norway | 107 | 106 | 90 |
| USA | 87 | 95 | 71 |
| Soviet Union (1956–92) | 87 | 63 | 67 |
| Germany | 78 | 78 | 53 |
| Austria | 55 | 70 | 76 |
| Canada | 52 | 45 | 48 |
| Sweden | 48 | 32 | 48 |
| Switzerland | 43 | 37 | 46 |
| Finland | 42 | 58 | 56 |
| East Germany (1956–88) | 39 | 36 | 35 |

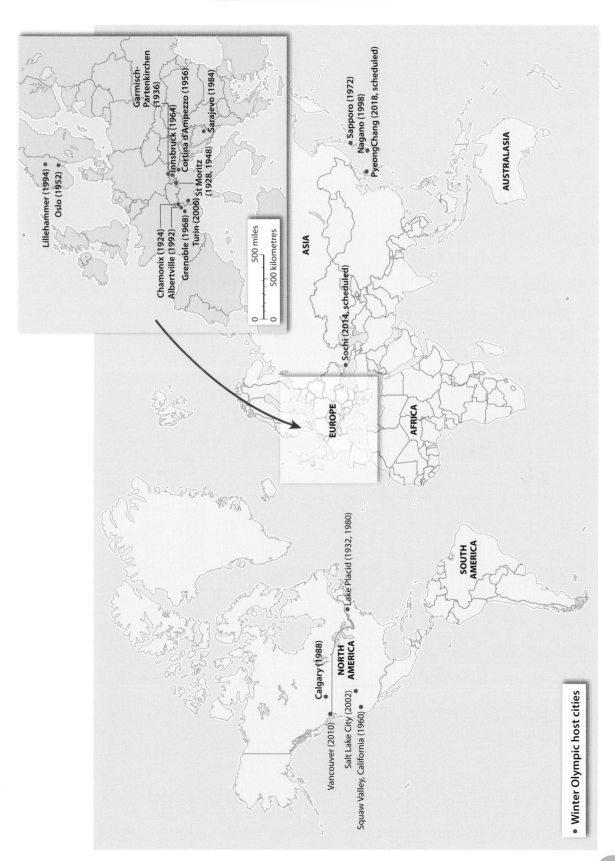

Lillehammer (1994)
Oslo (1952)
Garmisch-Partenkirchen (1936)
Innsbruck (1964)
Cortina d'Ampezzo (1956)
Sarajevo (1984)
Chamonix (1924)
Albertville (1992)
Grenoble (1968)
Turin (2006) St Moritz (1928, 1948)

Sapporo (1972)
Nagano (1998)
PyeongChang (2018, scheduled)

500 miles
500 kilometres
0
0

ASIA

AUSTRALASIA

Sochi (2014, scheduled)

EUROPE

AFRICA

Lake Placid (1932, 1980)

Calgary (1988)
NORTH AMERICA

SOUTH AMERICA

Vancouver (2010)
Salt Lake City (2002)
Squaw Valley, California (1960)

• Winter Olympic host cities

# Glossary

**artificial** made by people

**biathlon** winter sport that combines cross-country skiing and shooting

**bribe** illegal payment to someone in hope of receiving special treatment

**fibreglass** plastic that contains glass fibres to make it stronger

**halfpipe** half-moon shaped ramp used by snowboarders and freestyle skiers to perform tricks

**International Olympic Committee (IOC)** organization that runs the Olympic Games and decides where they will be held

**mascot** animals or cartoon figures used to represent each Olympic Games

**medal table** table showing which countries have won the most medals at the Winter Olympics

**Olympic Movement** all the people involved in the Olympic Games, including the International Olympic Committee, Olympic officials from each country, and competitors of each Olympic sport

**Paralympics** games for athletes with a disability, held after the Olympic Games in the same place

**professional** someone who is paid for doing something, such as playing a sport

**prosthetic** device that replaces a missing arm or leg, as used by some Paralympic athletes

**runners** steel blades on a bobsleigh

**Soviet Union** state made up of Russia and several neighbouring countries. The Soviet Union existed between 1922 and 1991.

**streamlined** designed to reduce air or water resistance

**toboggan** simple sledge used as a traditional form of transport in the Arctic

# Find out more

## Books

*Being a Pro Snowboarder* (Top Jobs), Cindy Klen (Wayland, 2012)
*Ice Hockey* (Winter Sports), Greg Siemasz (Raintree, 2013)
*Inside the Olympics*, Nick Hunter (Raintree, 2012)
*The Treasures of the Winter Olympic Games*, Olympic Museum
(Carlton, 2009)

## Websites

www.olympic.org
The website of the International Olympic Committee includes facts about
each Games and details of every Winter Olympic medal winner. The site also
features loads of photos and videos from Winter Olympic history.

www.paralympic.org
The International Paralympic Committee website includes information
about the Winter Paralympics, its stars, and opportunities to take part in
disability sport.

www.shaunwhite.com
This is the official website of Shaun White. Other Winter Olympic stars also
have websites and social networking pages. Official sites will give the most
reliable news.

If you want to try your luck at winter sports, search for the international
and national organizations in charge of the sport. Your national Olympic
Committee will also have information about who to contact.

# Index

alpine skiing (downhill skiing) 4, 12, 13, 20, 22, 23
artificial snow 27

biathlon 22
bobsleigh 7, 14, 15

Chamonix Games 6, 7
controversies 24–25
Crosby, Sidney 18
cross-country skiing 8, 12, 22, 24
curling 19, 22

disabilities, athletes with 22–23
drug cheats 24

figure skating 5, 6, 8, 16, 25
first Winter Olympics 6–7
freestyle skiing 5, 20

halfpipe 20, 21
host cities 26

ice hockey 7, 11, 18, 19
ice sledge hockey 22
International Olympic Committee (IOC) 5, 6, 7, 24, 26

Kerrigan, Nancy 24
Kim Yu-Na 16

luge 14, 15

mascots 11, 27
medal tables 7, 9, 19, 28

Nordic Games 6
Nordic skiing 12
Norway 6, 7, 9

Ohno, Apolo 17
Olympic Charter 5
Olympic flag 10
Olympic flame 10, 11
Olympic Games 10
Olympic Movement 5, 10
Olympic torch 11
opening ceremony 10, 11

Paralympics 22–23, 27
prosthetics 23

safety 20
short-track speed skating 16, 17, 24
skating 5, 6, 7, 8, 16–17, 24, 25
skeleton 14
ski jumping 13
ski-cross 5

skiing 4, 5, 9, 12–13, 20, 21, 22, 23, 24
slalom 12, 20
slopestyle events 20, 21
snowboarding 5, 20, 21
Sochi Winter Olympics 2014 21, 26–27, 28
speed skating 6, 7, 16, 17, 24
symbols 10

team sports 18–19

Vonn, Lindsey 12

White, Shaun 20
Woolstencroft, Lauren 23